Sweet Baby

Welcome to the World

By Flavia and Lisa Weedn
Illustrated by Flavia Weedn

Cedco Publishing · San Rafael, California

ISBN 0-7683-2151-4

Text by Flavia and Lisa Weedn
Illustrations by Flavia Weedn
© Weedn Family Trust
www.flavia.com

Published in 2000 by Cedco Publishing Company.
100 Pelican Way, San Rafael, California 94901
For a free catalog of other Cedco® products, please write to the
address above, or visit our website: www.cedco.com

Printed in Hong Kong

1 3 5 7 9 10 8 6 4 2

Book and jacket layout by Kathie Davis

The artwork for each picture is
digitally mastered using acrylic on canvas.

It is the

morning

of your

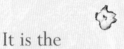

life,

sweet

baby...

and

all of your

dreams

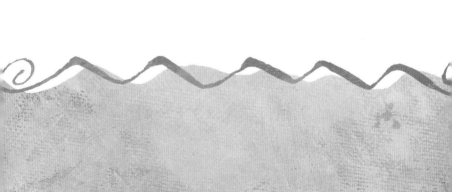

are just *beginning.*

Your *heart* is filled with *wonder,*

wonder

for you

are made

of lullabies and

love.

You have

no way

of knowing,

but you

hold all

of our

Tomorrows

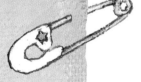

tenderly

in

your

hands.

You

are a warm

and wondrous gift

from the

heart.

Welcome

to the world,

dear

little one.

May God

bless

you

forever

and ever.